PIONEER GIRL

PIONEER GIRL

Maryanne Caswell

Illustrations by Lindsay Grater

Tundra Books

First published in Canada by McGraw-Hill Company of Canada Limited, 1964

This edition copyright © 2001 by Tundra Books, *McClelland & Stewart Young Readers*
Illustrations copyright © 2001 by Lindsay Grater

Published in Canada by Tundra Books, *McClelland & Stewart Young Readers*,
481 University Avenue, Toronto, Ontario M5G 2E9

Published in the United States by Tundra Books of Northern New York,
P.O. Box 1030, Plattsburgh, New York 12901

Library of Congress Catalog Number: 00-135770

Canadian Cataloguing in Publication Data

Caswell, Maryanne, b. 1873
    Pioneer girl

ISBN 0-88776-550-5

1. Caswell, Maryanne, b. 1873 – Correspondence. 2. Caswell family – Juvenile literature.
3. Frontier and pioneer life – Saskatchewan – Clark's Crossing – Juvenile literature.
4. Clark's Crossing (Sask.) – History – Juvenile literature. I. Grater, Lindsay, 1952-   .
II. Title.

FC3217.1.C38A4 2001   j971.24'202'092   C00-932714-2
F1060.9.C38A4 2001

Text taken from *Pioneer Girl* © 1964 by the McGraw-Hill Company of Canada Limited.

We acknowledge the support of the Canada Council for the Arts and the Ontario Arts
Council for our publishing program.

ONTARIO ARTS COUNCIL
CONSEIL DES ARTS DE L'ONTARIO

We acknowledge the financial support of the Government of Canada through the Book
Publishing Industry Development Program for our publishing activities.

Design by Terri-Anne Fong

Printed and bound in Canada

1 2 3 4 5 6   06 05 04 03 02 01

PREFACE

—

So on a misty, moisty morning
Kind of foggy was the weather,
Many friends assembled together.

Maryanne Caswell was fourteen years old on the gentle
spring day in 1887 when she wrote those lines to her grandmother. Maryanne, her parents, and her brothers and sisters
— Martha, Jen, Andrew, John, and Baby Mabel — were setting
out on a great adventure. Mr. Caswell had been a shopkeeper
in Palmerston, Ontario. He was about to take his family by
rail and oxcart to homestead on the wide prairie.

Maryanne had promised her grandmother that she would
write to her. And although she was often exhausted from the
journey — she must have written outdoors, or by candlelight,
or even by starlight — she kept her promise in letters that give
us an authentic picture of the life of a pioneer girl.

These were the times just after Confederation, when the
West was a landscape of dreams and promise. One by one
the provinces were forming: in 1869 Rupert's Land, owned
by the Hudson's Bay Company, became the Northwest
Territories. Manitoba became a province in 1870, and British
Columbia became a province in 1871. Saskatchewan, carved

from the Northwest Territories, became a province in 1905, along with Alberta. The great vastness would be linked together through telegraph and railway to create one nation.

For men like Maryanne's father, the west was where fortunes could be made, and the future was as boundless as the land. Moreover, the telegraph and the railway — vital lines of communication — needed communities to support them. Land was offered free to attract farmers. For a ten dollar legal fee and a promise to live on the farm for six months of each of the next three years, a man would be given a quarter section, or 160 acres, of land. James Caswell's three brothers had already been lured to the west. He was excited about following them.

Maryanne's letters tell a story of hardship, heartache, and great fun. She captures just the right details: dinners on the trail featuring a turkey who walks through the porridge, her disappointment at seeing the 'city' of Saskatoon for the first time with its fourteen drab buildings, and the endless landscape she would grow to love. Luckily for us, her Grandma Caswell kept the letters, dated from April 12, 1887 to January 1, 1888. When Maryanne was an adult and became Mrs. Thomas Hilliard, the letters were returned to her. They were published in the Saskatoon *Star-Phoenix* on September 11, 1952 and were published for the first time in book form by McGraw-Hill in 1964.

This edition of her letters brings her to life for a new generation of readers. Although she wrote many years ago, the humor, grace, and bravery Maryanne Caswell brought to her pioneer life make her a heroine for all ages.

April 12, 1887

Dear Grandma Caswell
and all our friends,

You had me promise to write you of our journey from Palmerston, Ont., to Clark's Crossing, or Saskatchewan P.O., N.W.T. I am trying to do so. Also I will not forget your request to help my parents all I can.

> So on a misty, moisty morning
> Kind of foggy was the weather,
> Many friends assembled together.

At the station were Knowles, Alexanders, Watts, Fawcetts . . . everybody near and dear. But the girls' lamentings and the misgivings of the old ones made us feel not so jubilant because it seems perfectly splendid to ride, eat, sleep on a train for a week. I assured them I would return for $37 if I did not like the enchanting, fairylike country to which we were going.

Martha pretended she was sorry to leave, and smeared her face. Now her conscience is troubling her. "All board," and we were assisted on board. Amid waving of hankies and

promises to write we left our pretty home town, the only
home we have ever known.

At Harriston we walked over a bridge to change trains
and again said goodbye to all our uncles and aunts and
cousins, for every one of them had come to give kindly aid
to father or brought gifts for our use on the journey. We
were loaded up with baskets, boxes of fruitcake, cookies,
maple syrup, "oop" sugar, cheese, ham and pickles.

At Orangeville we had to change trains again and meet
father who was with the "stock and settler's effects" train.
After placing us in our seats, mother got off to see father.
In the meantime the train moved and frightened us, for
what could we do with baby Mabel, no money nor tickets.
Frantically I told the conductor of our predicament. He
pulled a rope and had the train backed up to the platform.
Wasn't he kind? What joyous relief to see mother smiling

from the station. The sun was setting in shades of misty, smoky orange. We shall remember Orangeville.

This was our first night in an hotel. What thrills we girls had — a room and beds to ourselves while mother and the boys occupied a room down the hall. In the morning we felt as if we had not slept. Strange to hear the raps on the doors — a call to arms or a call to work was to begin. We dressed and went to mother, and then to breakfast. There were many guests at the Union hotel leaving for the great, wide, beautiful, wonderfully rich Manitoba, Red River and North West Territories . . .

All ready, we went for a walk and met father near the hotel. Again we gathered our parcels and were taken to another station by the lake. Then father took us to see Cousin Tom, city solicitor, then to his old friend Archibald Young who teased me about tumbling into the well for a cup the day he had come to visit us. I was an awful show that day.

He is going to help about a contract for supplies for the Mounted Police, and father is going to measure the Saskatchewan (river) between Saskatoon and Batoche for the best location for a railway bridge.

We waited patiently for our train as it was late. Then finally, a long, slow train came in with our car of stock and many similar cars for the passengers — immigrants we are. The seats and backs are wooden slats that can be pulled out, and the two facing and joining are used for a bed, which mother used. Then above, a large shelf is pulled down, and hangs by rods and hinges. This was our bed. There were a number of young men going to farm at Virden. One is Hayhurst's cousin, and one is Andrew Bell. They were kind and helped father carry the needed supplies for our comfort. Then there is a room at the end of the car with a stove to cook on and water. At the other end are washrooms. We were tired and glad to get into our shelf bed.

About midnight we began to move slowly. How delightful. At last to the land of dreams and enchantment – the train was our magic rug.

We halted; other passengers came in. Mrs. Naylor, her son and daughter are going to Manitoba. They were hungry, cross, and I guess tired. The boy wanted honey on his bread and it could not be, so he just howled. The little girl said, "Why can't ye take what ye git, and be thankful." The "git" amused us. They are nice people.

We awakened in a rough country covered with dirty snow, and to another dark day, the monotony broken by getting acquainted, meals, and playing when the train stopped. Father brought us fresh milk from the car.

The next day we travelled along Lake Superior covered with rotting ice. All about it were rocks and dirty snow. There were no houses nor people other than track men.

We'll soon be in Winnipeg, Grandma.

Lots of love, your

Maryanne.

Dear Grandma Caswell,

Mr. Willoughby and Mr. Fleming met us, and proceeding through the station we saw Winnipeg with horsepulled cars as in Toronto. There are two rails laid like the railway track. The cars are about ten to twelve feet long with the seats placed lengthwise. The horses are hitched to the end and when they want to turn they are put to the other end of the car.

Across a wet, muddy stretch of blackness, there were funny little black patched boxes against the horizon. These are tar-papered homes — black mushrooms like we played with in the woods. We walked across this windy stretch sometimes sticking (mired) on planks.

It was delightful to see again the big girls of our babyhood, grown up, keeping house. How mother and they chatted! We played, glad of the freedom.

Sunday noon we came to Portage la Prairie to see Uncle Ronald's (Martin) widow and children. It is wet and muddy but there are trees and a brick store, Garlands. We had dinner at Mrs. Smith's. Then we all got into a wagon driven by Jimmy Martin to go to their home five miles from Portage.

Along the road in the shelter of the clumps of bushes was snow. There were dozens of infected rabbits lying dead. Ugh! Disease infected them. We wondered why Uncle Ronald selected the farm so far away when he could have chosen from the surveying time (closer to town). Looks like park all about here.

Their house is of logs with two large rooms downstairs and four up. We saw great flocks of wild geese flying high like a great kite. Monday morning the boys shot three. They looked like an order of priests with their black collars and cowls. We had them for dinner. The boys were on the land and the girls were busy preparing for an evening party for us — our second party among grown-ups.

Everyone danced to the music of a fiddle, even the children, and had lots of fun swinging and going down the centre to the end. Two danced, one stepping up and the other backing away, and then coming forward again to quick music like birds on the lawn in spring. Finally we got tired watching others dance when we could not make any attempt, as we were not allowed to join in the fun. Where was the sin? But we had fun upstairs trying to dance until Aunt Catherine thought the ceiling might be loosened.

Tuesday we left this enjoyable home for Portage, the train, and home far beyond. At Burnside, the next station, I spied Mac on the platform as the train moved. We could not understand why, as we had said goodbye a few hours ago, until the conductor enquired if any of the ladies was "Aunt Mary." He had a parcel for mother that had been left at Aunt Catherine's — father's white shirt and Mabel's dress. The sun was hot, the train crowded, the country getting hilly and sandy but not a buffalo did we see . . .

Long after midnight we arrived at Moose Jaw and were met by father, who took us to the office of the land agent, Mr. Whitmore. Father had beds made for us on the floor, and we soon forgot the price of hotel rooms. Next morning we spent out-of-doors down by the creek, looking over the immigration shed where our goods were stored and above where people could lodge.

On a rise above the creek we saw our first Indian camp of teepees. We had permission to go to them. I was disgusted with the dirt but we seemed to amuse them for they smiled and laughed. In the afternoon we went down to Mr. Baker's store. There seemed to be anything one could possibly need. We had dinner with Mr. R. L. Alexander. The girls take turns in doing the different work. Nearly all the buildings are made of new lumber and not plastered walls. They shake in the wind, and the wind can blow here.

Mr. Alexander wants father to stay and not go on to Clark's Crossing. He is land agent and would get us settled on land and the girls of us could go to school. I would like to stay. Mr. Whitmore came to see us and had lunch. I am glad we are not in the large, cold, shaky immigration hall.

Uncle Joe sent a telegram from the government office at Clark's Crossing that the river at Saskatoon was impassable and that he was unable to meet us as arranged. The ferry was out. Father wants to get started Friday. He is making a rack for the wagon. We have two oxen, Buck, a white, and Berry, a roan. It is Thursday night now and we are ready to

start. Such an array of things as are being loaded on the wide rack.

The load included seed wheat, oats, potatoes, rhubarb, roots, lumber, kegs of nails, sacks of flour, ducks, chickens, turkeys in crates, food, bedding, clothing, a lantern and a pail hanging at the back and the iron wagon, with a box it is tied to. Mother and the children are to sit on top while I drive the cattle (first herd of Shorthorns brought into Saskatchewan) and sheep. We have Root's pure-bred collie, Brownie.

We got started in the afternoon of Friday. We had the company of Mr. Dick Richardson and Mr. Will Bate from Saskatoon. They had black and white oxen in harness like a horse while ours had a great, heavy wooden yoke. It is all so strange following a wagon track.

Toward evening we met Mr. Alexander again. He tried

to persuade father to locate nearer to Moose Jaw. He gave us an "A" tent in place of the round one we had. We camped near a slough. The oxen were unyoked and fed with the cattle near by. Mr. Bate put up the tent after we had made the fire, and helped get supper ready. It is strange and we do not seem to know what to do, but he is lots of fun, laughing and telling stories.

It seemed we had only gone to bed when we had to get up in the middle of the night and break camp in the grey, bleak dawn. Mother and the children were perched here and there on the load, while Martha and I were to drive the cattle around the slough further up. As we crossed the end I saw our oxen halted in the middle of a slough and heard haw-geeing, haw-gee. Then the children, one by one on Mr. Bate's neck, were carried to the dry land. We got around in time to see mother also being carried pick-a-back amid a lot of laughter.

The oxen, twisting in the soft mud to make progress, cramped the wagon and broke the axle. Father directed us all to make for a house in the dim distance, like a mark on the sky.

I'll tell all about it next time, Grandma. Everyone sends love.

Maryanne.

Dear Grandma Caswell,

(You remember that I told you how we got stuck in a slough and that father sent Martha and me – and the cattle of course – for help.)

So we gathered forces and started. Those Shorthorns would go any way but that way until Mr. Bate helped us. Then he returned to help unload the wagon to dry ground. We walked about an hour when we met a man driving a grey ox and a black horse hitched to a wagon. We, no doubt, looked as funny to him.

He stopped and asked us questions and very kindly told us to turn at a trail a few miles on. He was on his way to Moose Jaw for government seed. This team was all he had left from several. He talked to father and took mother and the children to his home, six miles back. Near the turn we met him again, on his way to Moose Jaw. When he arrived at father's place of plight he loaded the broken axle and took it to be repaired. The cattle, sheep, Martha and I got to the homestead about two o'clock, all tired out and hungry. Mother and our friend's bachelor uncle prepared dinner of savory wild duck.

Mr. Bate's wagon brought some of our belongings and then, much to our regret, he left us for Saskatoon. There were three rooms in this house, built of logs standing on end and mudded in the chinks. They are nice Englishmen.

Mrs. Heath, the mother of our kind rescuer, had died the previous winter and they are inconsolable in their loss. The small room is heaped a yard high with letters from England. I was sent to tidy it up but the uncle preferred to leave it in its present state. The room and belongings were those of his beloved sister.

Young Mr. Heath came home late Saturday night, or rather, early Sunday morning. He is returning to Moose Jaw and will bring the axle when repaired. It has been wet, bleak and windy all the week. We have helped mother in the house, read some English papers, herded the cattle, scanned the prairie horizon and walked into fields without fences. Mr. Heath made two trips for the axle before it was ready. We are to start in the morning and we are sorry to leave our friends.

In the grey, bleak, early dawn we prepared to start like gypsies as you can imagine. The sun appeared and the wind chased everything and smarted our hands and faces. About six o'clock in the evening we drove by a place where a young couple were camping in the log shell of a fair-sized unfinished, unchinked, doorless, floorless house while putting in their crop. The woman told mother of hard times and lack of food. They used four XXXX brand flour with syrup and that was all they had. We camped further on in a crimson twilight encircling a prairie sea.

Early Saturday morning we were on our way again, mother and the children under covers on the wagon, father with the oxen, and I following with the cattle and sheep.

Toward noon the sun had become very hot. Much to our delight we found our first prairie crocus, or wind-flower father calls them. The calyx consists of numerous, slender, silvery furred stems enveloping five petals of bluish mauve, quite similar to the tulips in our front yard. Their odor is just earthy, as if you were digging fresh moist earth. Mother was not so delighted as we were.

About two o'clock it got so hot the sheep panted and had to be urged and pushed on. Then we halted while father and mother proceeded to shear some of the sheep. The oxen lay down where they were, unyoked. After watering at a nearby slough our cavalcade, or motley procession, moved onward over the faded brown prairie. After sundown the wind came

screaming at us, the sky darkened and we were suddenly cold
as we had been hot. The sheared sheep shivered and bleated.

We camped hurriedly for the night near a great ravine
with hills on our left. We were near the valley of the Little
Arm. During the night the wind ceased, wearing itself out in
soft snow of six inches. Wet? I guess. All night father had
been in and out of the tent caring for some little lambs he
had found. They were so cold he wrapped them in his buffalo
coat and put them in the tent, too. We were all ready to
return to Palmerston with mother.

Sunday morning was quiet but everything and everybody
was soaked more or less. We stirred cautiously about our
limited space. Then the sun came out in all his splendour.
A wind rose and, presto, the snow was melting. The fowl in
crates were a woebegone mass of wet feathers so we let the
turkeys and ducks out, for we could catch them easily. Finally,
with a lot of trouble, a fire was started and porridge made.

We were about ready for 10 o'clock breakfast when some
men with horses and a wagon drove up. They were going to
Saskatoon and advised us to break camp as we would dry on
the road, and at the Little Arm (they) would be of assistance
in travelling across it. Just then the gobbler stepped into the
pot of porridge, so that spoiled our breakfast.

We all scrambled to get ready. The fowl were caught and
crated, the stock gathered and the tent and bedding spread
on the wagon to dry. Yes, our flags were flying in every available place. The lambs were put in the little iron wagon
attached to the big one, and the sheep followed more easily.

With the oxen yoked, and just at church time, we set out again. The snow was almost gone with the ground soaking wet and mushy. We followed the horse and wagon tracks around the hills, but there was no sign of the outfit.

We never did see them again, Grandma.

With love, from

Maryanne.

---

*D*ear *Grandma Caswell,*

A mile from our (Sunday) camping place father halted and considered the trail.

He called and said he would go ahead to test the footing and I was to lead the oxen after him. (This was an alkali flat in the valley of the Arm River.) When about 40 feet away he said, "Drive on." I pulled and haw-geed, but of no use. The oxen would not budge for me — "the gnat on the bull's horn."

Then I saw the oxen and wagon disappearing in the soft mud and yelled, and you know I can yell. Father came running back and all his efforts failed to move the outfit. The oxen were unhitched and pulled and driven and coaxed to extricate themselves. They did. Then the wagon-riders clambered down and ranged around while father, mother,

Martha and I laboriously unloaded and carried to safety the various things of the load.

A plank from the bottom was used as a lever under the hubs, with the keg of nails for a pivot. Finally about three o'clock we were out of the muck. The oxen, hitched to the wagon tongue, pulled the wagon out with much haw-geeing. We began to carry and reload for the third time.

Meanwhile the younger ones had been enjoying themselves rolling down the grassy hills, and we joined in the frolic. All too soon came the call to march again. Father protested the futility of Sabbath desecrations, for had we remained in camp we would have dried and rested and been at peace with God and ourselves and saved all this unnecessary labor. It was against his judgment to travel on Sunday. No one would persuade him again. And besides, the men had not waited to help us as suggested and arranged. He was truly annoyed and worn out.

About a mile on, Andrew and Jen discovered they had lost mitts so were sent back to look for them — "probably among those wolf willows." We were so terrified of seeing wolves pounce out and devour us. We found one mitt and ran all the way to the outfit.

After supper we moved on again. The sun was in a great blaze of yellow glory. The wind had fallen, sighing softly as in relief of duty done. We camped for the night while the world was pigeon blue and mauve. After singing of psalms and prayers — we have them almost as if we were at home — we were glad to snuggle down in our springless beds and listen to the frogs' orchestra.

Early Monday we were on the trail again. We have been so sleepy that we are promised that when we reach our destination we may sleep until we are satisfied. It was cold and the cattle were contrary, running any direction but the desired one. In exasperation I cried, and Martha was sent to help me.

About ten o'clock father went across the rise to the right and returned with a dry poplar pole, which had been cached the previous summer for an emergency. This was to do us for some fires, as no trees grew on this bleak yellow plain through which we would travel most of the day. It was broken only in places by buffalo trails and wallows. In these, the buffalo delighted to roll and dust themselves, or take a mud bath if it were wet.

We saw a few birds; one that sang heel-toe, and a one-two-three — like the dance at Aunt Catherine's. He is about as big, or more slender than a robin, flecked like a sparrow with a yellow vest, white collar and black tie — handsome. The sky was all plumy ruffles of rich mauves, crimson and orange, when we camped for the night.

How tired we were of walk, walk! The crocus, the wild geese with their honk, honk, the flap, flap of a covey of prairie chicken, have all lost their new charm for us. We fell asleep describing the pictures in the banks of clouds in the sunset. "A cloud lay cradled in the setting sun." We lay cradled on the greatest stretch of bare earth.

Tuesday father was astir early. Would he never rest? As usual, we had our drink of milk all round, the stock were gathered, the bedding rolled and hoisted on the wagon, the tent taken down, the children and mother placed here and there under the covers on the wagon and northward we go. The sun came up and promised us a good day so we sang, "Good morning, merry sunshine" and felt happier than for some days. We camped for breakfast.

After crossing a small gully, like a dry creek, we found some bright, shiny, dark green leaves with clusters of bright, hard red berries among them. It is a vine and the berries are stone berries. The crocus again delighted our hearts.

The country became more broken and varied yesterday's monotony that was so disheartening. What pleasant surprises might not be over the next rise! Father says we'll soon be near Saskatoon.

Love from everyone, Grandma,

Maryanne.

———◆———

*D*ear *Grandma Caswell,*

When Father cautiously informed us we might make the city of Saskatoon that weekend, how we skipped and danced and sang as we ran hither and thither after those contrary beasts.

In the afternoon it was down hills, up and always downward to a creek with a large sheet shining occasionally in the distance. Upon reaching the creek we camped. The animals wandered at will. We now had time and plenty of soft, clean accessible water, so a good wash was indulged in. Then away to view the wonderful and mighty Saskatchewan (river) from the farther hills — a beautiful, glistening sight with the bare rising plain beyond, completing the picture of the Saskatchewan elbow. I shall not forget it.

Mother cut seeds from the potatoes and cooked the remainder for supper, a change. The seeds will keep for days and be planted on our arrival. As we were about to dine so sumptuously, Gerald Willoughby — brother of Dr. Willoughby — came bouncing up with his team of spotted ponies on his return from Moose Jaw.

His trip evidently was disappointing for his wagon was almost empty. He was invited to join us in our evening meal. We finished the last of our fruit cake for dessert.

Mr. Willoughby offered to assist father up the long hill. This kindness pleased us all. We gathered forces for the march, the cattle unwilling to leave the succulent creek grasses. The horses were hitched with a chain and whiffletrees to our wagon tongue and then up, up, like King Bruce's spider we climbed, twisting here, turning there, up again. A halt was made to spell the panting oxen. Again a twist, an upgrade, a turn, a little run, a bit of urging and we finally made the top without any mishap.

As we rested on the top we refreshed our beauty sense with the beautiful scene. Far below, the shining waters were overcast, deepening to crimson with the gorgeous coloring of the sunset – light clouds flecked with king's yellow, changing to mauve and royal purple. Mr. Willoughby returned to the creek camp for his wagon. We all were proceeding when in a short time he overtook us, and soon he passed on.

Everyone was enjoying the unclouded moonlit scene refreshed by the clear fragrant air. Even baby Mabel was gay, amusing us with her sweet gooing to the moon and stretching her tiny arms to the old man of the moon. The irksome cattle followed, charmed, so I thoroughly enjoyed the respite. Each step brought the promised land nearer to our weary, lagging feet. Mr. Willoughby had wintered there, though we were not so favorably impressed with his story of how they spent the winter, and the school he taught, and Canaan where some of the boys fed cattle all winter.

However there must be something to lure him for he had gone to the railroad and returned through all this great, bare, solitary vastness. Maybe he has a girl.

We were now on a much travelled trail that led from the elbow to Batoche. It was quite different, with many ruts of traders, buffalo hunters and generations of Indians, to the former wagon tracks we had followed from Moose Jaw. We camped about nine o'clock in the most pleasant night we had spent in the open, with the earth for our bed and the sky overhead. Though the earth was hard we knew nothing of it until roused in the grey dawn to gather cattle while the bedding and tent were put on the wagon. The riders arranged themselves for their best comfort. A drink of milk, and we moved onward.

The day grew warm and windy. The country was black from fall prairie fires. We always halt for breakfast after we have travelled a few hours. About eleven o'clock we met a quiet-looking team of oxen driven by Mr. Elijah Cleveland – bulls he called them – on his way to Moose Jaw. He presented mother with some small teal ducks he had shot. We had them with more potatoes for our supper. It was a delicious change from bread, maple syrup, ham, eggs, fruit cake, milk and porridge. Father says it is a long time before we will tire of them again.

At noon today we camped beside a slough where the ducks had been shot. There was white stuff all about it, a kind of soda that burned our boots. Last summer it was so dry that the men and oxen were glad to have water that was left in the old tracks.

I was to bring the oxen to be hitched while mother and father finished shearing the sheep that had become tired of carrying their heavy fleece in the heat. While sitting on the front of the wagon idly playing with a pronged switch, I tried to see how close I could put it between Berry's toes. He jumped, Bright moved, the wagon rattled and father shouted "whoa!" Nothing more happened but father called "silly girl" to me. It was father's first time to be vexed with me.

Thursday, travelling was very tiresome. It was hot and the country was vast and bare except for grass, with never a break 'twixt earth and sky, just the straight horizon.

About four o'clock the country became more rolling and undulating and small poplar trees grew sparsely. Then down we went into a pleasant creek bottom. The cattle kicked up their heels and cavorted about and we ran to see our first black brick house. There was no one there and Mr. Wilson, the absent owner, had told father that we were most welcome to camp there.

I'll tell you all about it next time, Grandma.

Love from everyone,

Maryanne.

———◆—◆———

*D*ear Grandma,

We lost no time in looking the place (Mr. Wilson's black house) over. The house is of sod, plowed from the prairie about three inches deep, and piled like brick walls about three feet thick; there are two windows and a door and a roof of sod. The stable is built the same with poplar poles for stalls and mangers. It is a novelty but disappointing, nothing like Uncle Will Ross's white brick farm buildings. We are to have concrete ones, you know.

We made beds early. It is just camp, eat, prayers, sleep and up again, gathering cattle and sheep, rolling bedding, tucking in the riders comfortably after a drink of milk, on again, breakfast, on again, supper, on again, and camp for the night.

This night was still and cold. We heard weird screams, as if someone were getting hurt, but father said it was wolves howling. Why be afraid? Mother and father are next to the tent door. When gathering up early in the morning our axe, our valuable axe, was not in its usual place. It was found beside mother's portion of the bed where she had put it in case the wolves attacked us. Her alarm amused father.

In the grey, chilling dawn we had our usual refreshment of milk and made preparations to move on. The cattle, endeavoring to resist our best efforts to get them started, objected to moving from this good feeding ground.

We had been travelling about an hour when I sensed there was something unusual attracting father's attention. I was alert but could not discern anything other than the usual faded prairie grass. Then in the dim distance there was something moving. Buffalo? No. Indians? No. "Well, what is it?" I asked, but was answered only by a smile so I might not be too disappointed. "We will see."

The object drew rapidly nearer. A halt was made, the reins were thrown as a man jumped out of the wagon greeting father joyously, for men. Oh joy! It was Uncle Joe come to meet us.

After a survey of us, his team was turned about, I was hoisted to the wagon seat, given my first reins, told to drive and not get too far ahead. How elated I felt to drive the grey mare that had served Alex Caswell on the mission field in Dakota and later had carried Uncle Joe in rebellion times of 1885 to Battleford with a message from Saskatoon. Uncle Joe has told you he preferred to take a chance on his life rather than leave Grey to the Indians, and so he camped with his mare on the river bank for the river was impassable for her. You remember telling us, Grandma?

What an honor to drive horses and at the same time be relieved of those nuisances of Shorthorns! What care I if they are pedigreed and worth a lot of money! Uncle Joe now did the walking while I rode in state. At breakfast he told us that the ice had gone out of the river with a glorious bang and he had driven to Saskatoon to cross the ferry. He had

heard Willoughby's reports of us, and becoming alarmed, had driven on as fast as he could for we had been almost four weeks on the way and two on the trail. He thought we were apt to be short of food, but we had plenty.

Some of the load was transferred to my team and, of course, the riders. They wanted to drive, but nothing doing. The job was mine, though riding all day seemed long and tiresome.

Uncle Joe pointed to something in the distance, darker than the grass, and called them Cook's bluffs, about seven miles from Saskatoon, the place invested with many city wonders for us. We passed those bluffs on our right, although it looked in the distance as if we were heading into them.

SASKATOON!

Finally, about five o'clock we saw weird shapes dancing in the sun haze, and coming nearer, they proved to be houses, about 14 of them. Then we halted and to our bewilderment were told that this was Saskatoon. "But where is the city?" we asked. "On a map in the surveyor's office," was the reply.

What disillusioned, dejected girls we were, and so disappointed after this long trip to see only a city of 14, all kinds of stone, roughcast, plastered, frame, log houses, and sod, tin and tar-paper roofs. We did not care to move off the wagon, but Saskatoon citizens came out to greet us (some show) and to greet father, who had known some of them in his young days – G. W. Grant, J. D. Ponees and family.

I'll tell you more next time, Grandma. We're almost there.

Love,

Maryanne.

———— • ————

*D*ear Grandma,

Mrs. Trounce, the English lady whose husband kept a store (in Saskatoon) sent an invitation for mother to come to tea with her. So mother, Mabel and Jen stepped out to tea in the

best we had with us, while we lingered and then were escorted
to the ferry by all the men and boys and girls of the city of
Saskatoon. Why did we ever imagine it to be a city like
Toronto or Winnipeg?

The sun had gone down behind the clouds, the wind had
lulled. We all walked down the bank to the ferry, which held
the teams, oxen and horses and was pulled or poled over by
Mr. Stewart and the men folk. The water of the Saskatchewan
was dark brown and muddy looking, not brown and clear
like the Maitland. And so, up the bank with teams, cattle,
and sheep amid the chorus of good luck, promises to "look
us up" when located. One girl told us they had a team of
steers but intended to buy a team of "stallion-mares" when
they got rich. We wondered what breed she meant, but have
decided it was Clydes they intended buying.

We camped on a hill about a mile or more from the
ferry. We tried to make camp ready while the men took the
team and returned to bring mother and Jen. It was almost
dark when they arrived. Jen had been given some candy and
kindly kept a piece for us, but she said her hand was hot
and put the candy in her mouth to keep. We enjoyed the
laugh. We went to sleep, lulled by the singing of men in a
house nearby.

Through the night the wind wakened us and the dark
clouds of the evening just opened upon us and poured rain
in sheets. Then it settled to a good drizzle for the day. Mr.
Horn came to have us take shelter in the nearby house which
we gladly did. It seemed full of men getting pancakes ready.

What a funny place! The house is built of poplar logs or poles standing upright, with two doors, back and front, four small windows, unpainted floor and bare log walls. Sacks of oats and wheat did for seats, along with two homemade chairs, a stove, table and bed. The men were nice, kind and jolly, so life here could not be so awful. (This was Brown and Will Horn's combination house, built so that half of it was on each quarter section.)

Mother got breakfast on the stove, and as the rain ceased it was decided we would move on. We were all put into the horse wagon with instructions that Fan was to be made to keep up her end of the whiffle-tree, and a message for Uncles John and Rob. I was given the lines and told to follow this well-beaten trail of many ruts until we came to our destination. We could not miss it, the only habitable place on the trail. The men would be late arriving as the stock were tired.

At the big ravine it had almost ceased to rain. We let the horses feed a bit but did not span out for Grey might make for home and leave us. Of course we squabbled as to whose turn it was to drive. Now we are on the last stretch of the trail to Clark's Crossing from Moose Jaw, our last camp for a while unless we return with father.

About this last camp we found several places enclosed with a ring of stones and wondered where the children were who had played house with these rings. We had not heard a voice or seen anything from Buffalo Lake to Saskatoon. Though we heard a man and his daughter had a ranch at the Elbow, we did not see them. After a little run to stretch, a bit of lunch, we climbed the wagon and commenced the last stage of our long, long journey, four weary weeks, lacking a day.

How good home will be to us! Miles and miles, days and days of land, thousands and thousands of 160-acre homesteads and pre-emption land. "We cannot have one of those."

About four o'clock we saw a man away in the distance, nothing else except for birds, frogs and gophers — something like squirrels but not so pretty. When we came up we found the man was our dear Uncle Rob who had sighted us and come across a mile or more to give us welcome. We were indeed glad to see him again and hear him jolly us on how we had grown.

He had left his plowing or would have come on to Uncle John's with us and taken us home with him. Uncle John lives by the side of the trail, has a fenced garden enclosing trees and fruit shrubs, and a front gate on the trail. We drove around to the yard and were welcomed by Uncle John and Aunt Patience quite fondly. Albert peeped shyly from behind his mother's skirt. We have a half mile further north to go but are to stay here and at Uncle Rob's until lumber is brought from Moose Jaw.

When the men and team and stock arrived we had supper, fried potatoes, bread, butter, eggs, no jams, jellies, fruit, syrup or cake. We are hungry for home and Palmerston. Uncle Rob came for mother and father, Mabel, Andrew and Jen — John to stay with Martha and I at Uncle John's.

Sunday morning I was taught to fold (the bedclothes) from the floor without holding each piece. We have inspected your sod shanty across the trail, Grandma, and hunted to make sure you did not leave any of the pictures you had hidden from the rebels two years ago.

Aunt Patience had an organ, which she played, and we sang hymns. Then we went over the ravine to Uncle Rob's and met Aunt Frankie. She is very nice and prim and kind. She played with us in the ravine where we went for water for supper. Wallace is lots of fun. He is learning to talk.

We reluctantly returned to Uncle John's watching a beautiful sunset of sheets of orange and mauve. The prairie seemed to be on fire.

Monday everybody was given work to do and we were to help. Uncle Rob plowed for Uncle John and sowed the White Russian seed wheat father had brought. We planted the potatoes on our own land — or it will be our own if we stay on it for three years — and the rhubarb and currants were planted also on last year's breaking. I wish we could live close to the river.

Good night, Grandma.

Love to you from

Maryanne.

May 8, 1887

*D*ear *Grandma,*

(Here we are in Clark's Crossing.) First day was Sunday.
We were awakened from our promised long sleep, that there
was no room to move till we had folded our bedding. We
dressed and were shown how to fold and put our bedding
out of the way.

Uncle John made flour porridge. Aunt Patience fried eggs
in lard with bread. We had breakfast. After helping to wash
the dishes and learning how to feed calves from a pail in

which we were to coax the calf to drink after inserting our fingers in its mouth, we were glad to sing hymns to Aunt Patience's playing on the organ she had brought from Cherokee, Iowa.

By and by, Martha and I, wearying for mother, stole quietly as we could to Uncle Rob's where the others of the family had slept and were to stay until we had our own shelter, as it might be.

The ravine was lovely in its dips and curves deepening to the river, the water pleasantly gurgling on its way in the evening shadows. Aunt Frankie, with Wallace, met us at the top. Our family had rushed down to us at the bottom. We like Aunt Frankie. She is kind and pleasant to us. We had a dainty supper, helped wash up, then played skipping stones with the children on our way to the river. Neither Wallace, nor Uncle John's Albert can talk yet, though they soon will have made friends with us quite readily.

Uncle Rob's house is of small, white upstanding poplar logs, plastered and whitewashed, two large rooms, bedroom and pantry. Uncle Rob has made a bed-sofa, stool and side-board for the parlor, very pretty cut-work and comfortable. He has not been with the government telegraph company since the "Rebellion." He, it was, sent the message from Duck Lake of the rebellion to General Middleton in the east. While out repairing the cut telegraph line he was taken prisoner by the rebels and placed in a cellar in Batouche's house in the village of Batoche. Later he was liberated through the intercession of Louis Ross, a half-breed who was also taken prisoner with him while repairing the telegraph line.

Next week was a busy one for each of us. Father sowed his White Russian wheat on his last year's breaking; the peas, oats and flax on Uncle Joe's land. I was shown how to handle the oxen, to harrow a good seed bed while father sowed from a big bag tied round his waist. All went well till I came to the end of land, turning too short the harrows tipped up on the oxen's back, frightening them into a run. I hung on to the rope halter shouting "whoa" till father came to release the harrows, explaining the serious effect to us if the oxen had gotten out of control. My hands were burnt with the rope. Mother made a salve of Balm of Gilead (black poplar) to heal my blisters.

With willing help and hindrance, we assisted mother to plant the roots of rhubarb, currants, strawberry, iris, and others we had brought with us from Palmerston. The garden seeds got under the ground. Our food to prepare, the care of Andrew and Mabel, many new chores to learn, the wandering cattle to herd as they wander far, and helping father get ready for a trip to Moose Jaw (for supplies), gave us no time for repining and wishing we had stayed at Heath's out from Moose Jaw, or, as Mr. Alexander tried to persuade father, remained nearer the railway.

When looking for the cattle beyond the north ravine, we saw an ox-team with wagon standing in the slough. They had run away with their owner, Mr. Mears, an Englishman, on his way from Saskatoon to Prince Albert. He was soaked to the hips, trying to coax the stubborn, difficult beasts out. He told us where the cattle were, and as later we drove the cattle to Uncle John's kraal, we heard singing. The ox-team was tied to the fence, and bedding spread out to dry. Aunt Patience was at the organ, Mr. Mears in scanty attire was singing rustily, "Bringing in the Sheaves" – with us it was bringing home the cattle. They sang "Pork and Beans and Hard Tack," the "Pembina," "Red River Girl." Aunt Patience sang, "There is nothing in this World but Trouble and Dirt."

They were having fun, though.

Love from all of us,

Maryanne.

———— ◆ ————

*D*ear *Grandma,*

On Monday, father with the oxteams, Bright and Berry, Uncle Joe's Cap and Major, and horses Fan and Grey, were ready to start on the long trail (back to Moose Jaw). I was sent to see the cause of the delay. Here was Uncle Joe with his feet in a bucket of hot water – like Samantha Allan's surprise party – preparatory to putting on white wool socks mother had given him. In his humorous way he explained he was afraid if he fainted on the trail someone might pull off

his socks to revive him and he would like to know his feet
were presentable when tickled. Whom might you meet in
200 lonely, lonely miles? "They will soak your head, not your
feet." Soon they got started on their long trip for lumber,
food and household goods.

Uncle Rob also left for Battleford, with Polly, his lone
mare, hitched to a stone boat to slide over the prairie grass.
He went to see about a government contract. Said Wallace
would be "talking like a whale" when he returned.

We went to the river with mother to cut green willows to
make baskets, which we would need to hold and carry things,
and a large basket for Mabel's bed or cradle. We had a bath
while there, enjoying it much.

Mother showed Aunt Frankie how to make soap. She
used a large kettle set on stones over a fire out from the
house. They had run lye from a barrel of ashes but it was
too weak so they put lye from a can, too, with bits of fat and
grease in water to boil, stirring it from time to time. While
it was cooling they put in a cup of precious coal-oil, a piece
of copperas. Then it looked like mottled castile soap.

We went to the river for more willows for baskets and to
make a splintbroom for sweeping. There was a boat hauled
up on the stones. Two queerly dressed men in fur caps with a
foxtail hanging down the back were cooking at a campfire.
They were pleasant, friendly fellows and seemed glad to see
us. They were trappers and were having beaver for supper.
They offered us a bit of the tail. It tastes like soft, soft

gristle. The beaver fur is beautiful like silk down with long, protecting hairs.

We have the incubator set at Uncle Robs, which is the only available place.

On Sunday, Uncle John took Aunt Frankie, Jen, Martha and me to Clark's Crossing Post Office across the river in a small boat he had made. He showed us how to help with a paddle, warning us not to try the boat when alone as the current would sweep us away to destruction.

Mr. and Mrs. J. F. Clark have the P.O. There is no ferry here for Clark's Crossing now because the ice swept the ferry away down the river in the spring freshet of ice going out in fresh chunks. The stage brings the mail to Batoche from Qu'Appelle on the way to Prince Albert. From Batoche a man with a buckboard and pony carry the mail to Clark's Crossing and Saskatoon every second Tuesday, returning to Batoche on Wednesday. Mrs. Powe is Saskatoon postmistress. Mr. Clark asked us to stay for dinner. We had potatoes, fried eggs, bread, butter, jam — raspberry — and some tea. My appetite shamed me when Mrs. Clark said, "Another loaf of bread, J. F." He reached to a boiler behind him and passed a loaf which Mrs. C. cut. Since I have been teased that I eat so heartily I am thin. Mother says, "an active, whistling girl and jumping sheep are the best stock a farmer can keep" though father does not approve of girls whistling.

The evening was soft and warm when we returned. Indeed, the days have been lovely, warm and sunshiny.

Evenings of gloriously hued sunsets, frogs trilling mono-
tonously from the sloughs, a shypoke or bittern croaking
ger-umph as if a saw were being filed – to sharpen – in his
throat. Try saw-setting and you will know.

On the 24th of May we took all the children to hunt eggs
from stray fowl. Johnny called us to see the pretty black and
white kittens he had found. The big ones came in view waving
black and white plumes, and having heard of their perfume we
sped away carrying Wallace and Albert as best we could. –
Anyway skunks or not, it was a good holiday.

We have butter now as mother made a wooden lid for a crock and a dasher to churn. It is much better than shaking cream in a jar, or as the Israelites did in a goat-skin. We also have maple syrup. Mother boiled potatoes in their skins using the drained water. She added a little sugar and boiled to a syrup. Very good, but not so good as Uncle Will Ross makes in his sugar bush.

We're all fine, Grandma.

Love, from

Maryanne.

———————◆———————

Dear Grandma,

We have (just) planted sacks of potato cuttings, mother keeping part of the potato for food. Uncle John drove a team of black and white steers — that have strayed here — to plow furrows. We put the cut side of the potato down against the edge of the furrow. They have to be straight. Then the next furrow covers the potatoes.

While we were doing this at Uncle John's, Andrew, who has not been well, stood at the end of the garden patch. Enviously Wallace Donnan threw a clod, which struck Andrew in the middle. We had sort of a warm time when Andrew screamed and doubled up. We took him to where mother was cutting potatoes. Later he returned.

Again he was taunted and dared to lift a sack of cuttings. We yelled not to do so, too late to prevent him trying. In a few minutes he vomited blood. Then mother carried him to Uncle Rob's where Aunt Frankie and mother did all they could within limited medical means.

The Molloys from the telegraph office, which is on our side, west of the river opposite Clark's Crossing, brought some brandy. Uncle John and Aunt Patience also came to discuss matters. On Saturday morning we were truly glad to see Uncle Rob in the distance on a stone boat gliding over the sunlit prairie. We ran to meet him with our news.

Quickly he took in the situation and headed for the telegraph office to arrange for a man with a good team to meet father and Uncle Joe on his way from Moose Jaw with loads of supplies to urge him to come with all possible speed. Telegraph repair men Archie Brown and Ted Harrington with their team of horses and buckboard went to meet father at Saskatoon while they, with Uncle Joe, brought on the teams. Andrew was happily conscious when father arrived Sunday. He smiled wanly and asked father to pray. Later it began to drizzle and continued for several days. Early Monday, Andrew spoke to us for the last time.

Tuesday afternoon we buried him in a small coffin Uncle Rob made and covered with white embroidery which Aunt Patience gave to use. On our quarter-section we all stood about repeating together the Lord's Prayer led by Uncle John.

We put some stones about him, one dark, mottled grey with fern-like marking at his head. Sorrowfully, with heart-broken parents, we turned to resume our several duties with a determination to do all we could courageously to help them.

The oxteams arrived with our lumber stored in Moose Jaw and food supplies from Palmerston. Uncle Joe had arrived earlier in the week with the horses. Archie Brown, who was repair man from this point, Clark's Crossing, during the rebellion, reported the wagon wheels became so rickety and loose on the rim that the wheels had to be taken off and soaked in a slough in order to carry on. It was not always so easy to locate a camping spot for this purpose.

He had been in charge from Wilson's, at Beaver Creek, where he met the teams. Uncle Joe, with the horse team, left the ox-brigade and hurried home. We now have a wagon with a wooden leg and tires of other wheels wrapped in shagginappy — cowhide soaked in water till it is soft and pliable. Telegraph wire is used in repair work too, for which the men are thankful. What a lot of unloading and reloading in those 200 lonely, uninhabited miles.

The men have built a shanty or shack for us with the lumber intended for our house, which will be built as soon as possible. The kiln is already in the ravine with wood cut sufficient to burn the limestones, which father prepared last year, 1886, when he brought cattle to Uncle John and Uncle Joe. They built the shanty by putting poles in the ground and nailing the boards, one side above the other to slope the roof. Beds were of poles driven into the ground, boards at one end, and side and bottom. We filled the cotton ticks with prairie hay. Sheets for partition. Uncle Rob made a table and benches of poles in the ground, and boards for the top, so with a stove and prairie grass for a carpet we established our homestead.

(You can guess we're happy to have a place of our own.)

Love, from

Maryanne.

*D*ear Grandma,

Uncle Rob left for Prince Albert this week. We found some
wild goose eggs about five miles west of us and have put
them under a hen with the hope they will hatch — which
three of them did and we made pets of them.

We are digging a well. Uncle Joe digs the blue clay from
the well hole into a wooden bucket, which hooks on from a
long rope through a high pulley trip. The other end of the
rope is attached to whiffletrees on the oxharness traces.
The ox pulls, father empties the bucket and backs the ox,
thereby lowering the buckets to Joe who shouts, "Look out."

On Sunday, while up on the roof with a telescope to
locate the cattle, we spied a sort of dun colored animal running hurriedly this way. We presumed it was a deer as we
had not seen anything like this out of a picture book. Jen
asked if it would be a sin to run it into the kraal and wait
till Monday to shoot it for meat. Father's answer was a non-
committal grin. Our "deer" was Uncle Rob's brindle cow
on the run home to her calf. We had an idea where to look
for the cattle later in the day.

We had Sunday school, as we called it, the uncles and
aunts joining us for a sing-song of psalms and hymns.

Father had turned the oxen loose, thinking they would feed
with the other cattle. When we brought the cattle home there
were no oxen, though we searched far and wide for them on

horse-back and with field glasses. Father was quite dismayed. Mr. and Mrs. Molloy of the telegraph station, who had come to visit us for a little while, kindly offered to lend us their pony, Mark, and the buckboard. So it was arranged that father was to ride the blind, black pony to the north, while mother in the buckboard would drive west until she met father.

On Monday, not a happy looking day, they set out, father north and mother west. We kept ourselves busy. Toward evening father returned tired and unsuccessful. When informed mother had not returned his face reflected dire fear.

We were shocked at the grievous situation that faced us. Urging us to pray, father hastened to Uncle Joe's to give the alarm, and on to Molloys to have messages sent to Henrietta and Battleford telegraph stations to be on the lookout for mother. Our mother, lost on the great lonely prairie with Henrietta station the only habitation in 100 miles.

Three men from the telegraph station, and the uncles, joined father with all available cow-bells and guns just as darkness came on, without a moon or star in the sky to break the bleakness of the night wind. We were in a panic at the thought of mother's worried condition, for father kept saying frantically, "She's lost, she's lost. Mary, terrified, will lose her reason. Oh, why did I ever come so far from civilization?" We had never known father so distracted.

The dark, windy night wore on. We ground and made coffee of roasted barley that mother had done in the oven to take the place of real coffee – the men had to refresh themselves as they came in, as arranged, to report. Our hearts ached of the terrible calamity without mother. Life just could not go on. Jen developed an earache, Mabel could not understand. John bravely kept the fires burning. Martha and I took turns going out to listen for wind messages to end our terrible suspense.

In the cold, grey dawn we were intensely relieved to hear voices and later to see our dear mother's pale, though smiling, face. So happy that a possible tragedy was averted, we kissed her trembling lips almost to pieces as she recounted the previous day's experiences. Travelling west, she had not found the Battleford-Carlton trail until later than calculated. Then going north, and not meeting father or the oxen, she decided to retrace her steps before the fading light obscured the tracks.

After she had left the cart-rutted trail, she recollected they had not stopped to feed all day. Now anxious to make the most of the waning light, she urged the pony till finally he stopped near a small bluff of trees to eat. When she had loosened him from the shaft, she tied him with the lines to the wheel to feed, (and) worry and cold began to bother. Without matches for a fire, she stood by the pony for warmth and company. What if he should get away in the darkness? Feeling drowsy she sat in the buckboard and was later startled to hear strange sounds of guns and bells. Thought she must have fallen asleep and dreamed. Then the pony whinnied. She realized that the gun-fire was to attract attention, not wild Indians attacking. The men finally heard her shouts, rescued her, and rejoicing brought her home to us with all possible speed.

After breakfast prayers, father had a special one of grateful thanksgiving for dear mother's safety.

It was all pretty exciting, Grandma.

Love, from

Maryanne.

*D*ear *Grandma,*

(The oxen are all right.) Later in the week the Henrietta telegraph operator, Mr. Salisbury, informed us the lost oxen were halted on the trail to Battleford, for which we were all relieved and thankful.

We were sorry to know that Mrs. Trounce, the lovely English lady who had invited mother to come and have tea with her while we were passing through Saskatoon, had died. Mother regrets that she could not go to her in her extremity. The children are going to England with their father.

A peddler, Mr. Davidson, with a team of grey ponies and buckboard, called to see us. His beautiful black and white dog chased our sheep out of sight. We have not even seen their tracks.

Our first mail from Palmerston brought a letter that Grandfather Martin, mother's father, had died suddenly and changed his will just a short time before. Mother is hurt and inconsolable; father disappointed. We were, too, for had it not been for an innocent remark of mine, grandfather's parting gift of money to mother would have been much larger and meant more comforts and a musical instrument for us. I am truly sorry as we will not get a cash payment on the Palmerston property till fall or spring.

A Prendergast boy on a black horse called on his way from Prince Albert to Saskatoon where his Uncle George Horn lives on the rise where we camped. He told us he had seen our lost sheep about ten miles north but they bounded away at his approach.

Father has made a cart of two iron wheels, the wagon seat on springs fastened to the axle, poles for shafts, shagginappy for harness, clothesline rope for reins, so that two or more of us can ride to hunt the pesky, roaming cattle. We have learned to ride horseback on the blind black pony, which, with a pretty little colt, came as strays to Uncle Joe's. It must have been lost a long time and out all winter, judging from its shaggy-haired patchy coat.

We wear blue indigo denim dresses, sunbonnets and our measured, strongly handsewn shoes or boots, made in Palmerston. The wiry prairie grass cuts into anything a bit fine or soft. The spear grass wiggles in to stay unless pulled out.

We had a pleasant treat when a number of red-coated North-West Mounted Policemen came galloping to our domain on their way to Saskatoon for some military manoeuvres to keep them fit. They are nice, polite Englishmen looking smart on their beautiful mounts with fresh accoutrements and trappings. Their commander and father drank the health of "Her Gracious Majesty, Queen Victoria" in buttermilk. The wagons and their dunnage came altogether too soon for us as we were enjoying the novelty of the brilliant company, and the superb symmetry of the well-groomed, prancing horses of the North-West Mounted Police.

The first of July, Dominion Day, dawned bright and gay. So were we, for had we not been promised a holiday with mother at the river? Quickly the chores were done. Harnessing Berry ox to the stoneboat, leaving Bright for Uncle Joe and father at the well, we loaded the big iron pot, wash-tub, soiled clothes, pails and barrels with our lunch aboard and off we happily set to the foot of our place at the river to fish, wash and play.

We built a fire between the stones, set the pot on it full of water to heat while we scampered about. We found a great pile of buffalo bones where the bank drops steeply to the river, stones, trees and shrubs below. Long ago there must have been a stampede for the countless buffalo skeletons

heaped high as ten-twelve feet from a madheadlong rush over
the sharp bank indicates this is how they met their death,
or the earth gave way under them. There are lots of buffalo
paths to the river.

In a thorn bush nearby we found a hawk's nest with two
young ones in it. Carefully we picked them up by the wings.
Jen, being too close to peek into the nest, got her face
scratched from their claws as they swooped toward her.
While playing in the coarse gravel we were richer by pieces
of petrified wood and a bit of petrified fish about two inches
long. I have it yet.

When we returned, the water was ready so we helped
wash the soiled clothes, and the sheep's wool for carding,
later had a bath, hung the clothes to dry on the bushes while
Jen and John attended to the fish lines. After a bit of lunch
we hunted for berries, hopped on the stones and occasionally
ran to the top of the bank slope road to keep an eye on the
cattle, which we had driven with us. We caught seven small
fish, keeping two for father and Uncle Joe. We cleaned and
fried the five for our picnic supper with cookies with a raisin
in the centre for a treat.

Love from us all,

Maryanne.

*D*ear *Grandma,*

(Our picnic was just over when) Aunt Frankie, who had been in Saskatoon, joined us and to get Jen to stay with her until Uncle Rob returned. We gathered the washed clothes filled the barrel with water in the rays of the setting sun; up the bank for home, herding the cattle along. The sky was memorably beautiful in its orange, crimson, purple and mauve tints of vivid colorings as superb and warlike as the battlefield of Honenlin blending, fading, reflecting to the water of the beautiful, swift Saskatchewan resplendent in the unappreciated silence.

The mosquitoes were terribly vicious and as we neared home Berry became unmanageable, broke from me, upsetting and scattering the pots, pails, laundry and water barrel. So ended our first of July, 1887.

During the night the rain came in torrents. The knotholes of the roof-boards leaked and rivers flowed inside and out. Mother, as she frequently had to do, put pots and pans on the beds to catch the drips. We dared not move the least bit or water is spilt. The quilts take such a long time to dry thoroughly hanging on poles of the garden fence and this hot, golden sun burns and fades them very much.

The weather is so hot that the heat in the distance dances like wild Indians riding to battle. The prairie is transformed into an enchanted land, inhabited by elves and fairies. If you listen carefully to the whispering of the wind in the grass, the buzzing of the insects about the countless bright, lined flowers, changed by a miracle every few days to another color and variety, you are in another world.

We have gathered, dried and pressed many of them. A great variety of vetch as in Gray's Botany, which Uncle A. K. gave us years before we left home. The first to show were crocus or mauve anemones in their fur coats. Very much like tulips, then clusters of purple violets, orange cowslips, yellow pea blossoms on a long stem, several kinds of tufts of purple not unlike a thistle, a low vine of coral hollyhock blossoms. Wild tomatoes, but they taste as if you held a copper penny in your mouth; ground plums, magenta, shooting star, blue gentians, blue stars on the grass, dainty bluebells create a haze of blue all about; roses galore, white and blue asters, golden-rod in three different kinds, wild sage with purplish pink burgamot, white yarrow, wormwood, pink, fireweed. Dainty Indian paint-brushes along the river ravines, an occasional Indian moccasin, yellow and pink ox-eyed daisies here and there interspersed with wild, strongly-scented candytuft.

For future use we gathered wormwood for use as poultices to reduce swellings, wild sage and onions for seasoning, anise with its long, purple licorice-odored spikes for cough medicine, tansy and yarrow for yeast, golden-rod for dye.

A plant with three stiff silvered leaves – like clover – with purplish blossoms, the root of which when dried and cut makes splendid gunwads for the muzzle loaders father uses. The beauty and variety of these, each in their turn make a

marvellous dainty and gaudy carpet, very pleasing to the eye,
especially when you look to the west about sunset to see the
most wonderful colorings of blue, orange, crimson flames
splashing across the whole horizon sky from north to south.
We marvel at its varying beauties and wish we had paints to
try to transfer the vivid and dainty shades to something
other than heart's memories.

Mother made cheese this week as it was so hot. We have
more milk as the cattle do not wander quite so far away.
The milk is warmed, the rennet — a calf's stomach — put
into it. These we had brought from Palmerston. When the
rennet has thickened the milk to junket it is cut up to drain
the whey off, then left to ripen. To test it mother took a
heated poker and touched a bit of the curd to it; if it
threaded it was ready for salting. Then kneaded and pressed
into a cheesecloth sack into a small half-keg with holes in
sides and bottom. A plate and stones on top of this keg is
put between two planks at either end of which is wrapped a
chain. As the cheese is pressed, the hook of the chain is
moved to increase the pressure. Occasionally the cheese is
turned till drained of whey, then buttered to preserve it till
ripened and used.

We have been down along the river for miles, scanning
and searching for the body of little Harry Molloy, but did
not find it. The Molloy children were playing in bare feet
down the river in the sand. On the run home little Harry
was last in line. Evidently he was too close to the water-edge
for his footprints showed where he had slipped into a large

hole. We are very sorry for them. Also for the drowning of
the nice Prendergast boy off the scow at Saskatoon. His
mother and sisters are on their way here from England.
What grief awaits her.

About six miles down and near the river not far from
scraggly bushes we know as "the horse" we found several
Indian graves. They were heaped with stones, larger and
smaller. It must have been hard work to roll and carry these.
We peered and pried and tried to move to see beyond down
among the stones hoping of course to find an Indian relic.

Nearby were several circles of stones within a large circle.
The Indians must have camped here for some time as deep
camp-fire spots have burned into the ground almost large
enough to crouch into. A few dried twisted poplar stumps
remain, which someone twisted while green. Not far away I
found a long sharp-pointed peculiar looking knife. The
blade and handle appear to have been welded by hand. The
handle is of open-work copper with crumbled bone underneath. It has lain there a long time. Looks very much like
Grandfather Martin's dirk. Who has been here and lost this
knife? Though lying for years it is still very sharp and not
eaten with rust, truly a good knife.

We also found several stones with grooves cut all round
the centre about three-quarters of an inch deep. Stones are
oblongs or ovals about the size and shape of a large, good
egg. These are no doubt war clubs or hammers to sling
about from a strap. Down by the river, almost screened by
the bushes, we found an old scow high and dry on the

stones. Evidently it had been carried out from some place and lifted by ice in spring flood, drifting in the lowered water to its lonely fate far from its moorings, possibly Medicine Hat, the nearest ferry or scow place beyond Saskatoon.

It makes you wonder about lots of things.

Love, from

from *Maryanne*.

———— ◆ ————

*D*ear *Grandma*,

We have been to Molloys (today) for the mail and with eggs, as they are glad to have what we can spare. The yokes are very yellow, not because the fowl are pure Black Spanish but because of the many grasshoppers they feed on. The hoppers have eaten in on the grain about ten to 20 feet, at the edge it is eaten quite clean; though Aunt Patience says it is nothing compared to the hopper destruction in Iowa when she was a girl. We have picked and dried at least a bushel of raspberries and a cotton grain-sack of saskatoon berries. They taste and look like tiny or small purple apples.

The gophers are little scamps. They are about the size of an Ontario rat (of which we have none, thanks be); the color of the yellowed grass; not unlike a squirrel, but not such a fluffy tail. They burrow into the ground and have numerous holes or doors into and out of their dens. When startled or you approach they sit on hind legs very still. One could mistake them for a tethering stake. Then they dive into the hole and pop out of another to learn the news.

We have to snare them about the garden as they are too fond of vegetables. We got one that had black barley but there is none that we know of unless 25 miles down and across. They no doubt travel. We use leather shoe strings in a loop or noose set it over the hole, and as Mr. or Mrs. Gopher pop up we quickly pull the string and there is Mr. Gopher squirming in the loop. John and Jen have become quite expert in snaring. There are plenty of them and no good to us.

Mother made some yeast-cakes before all the cornmeal would be used. These with the berries dried in the sun take some attention and turning to get them just right so they will not mildew.

For the yeast-cakes she boiled buttermilk, and stirred in cornmeal, ginger, and 3-4 yeast cakes from Ontario, kept warm, and then more meal to roll, cut and dried in the open air.

It is haying time, so out into the great, unbroken, western expanse of prairie for ten or 12 miles father and I started with our ox-team hitched to the wooden-legged wagon, with mower knives, rake, forks, camp equipment and food for a week's stay. Father had not been very well. I was to be company and cook for the camp. This did not seem enough for me in the loneliness so after cutting some of the hay I was shown how to turn the winnows with a long pole that the other side of the cut hay might be exposed to the sun to cure. Then how to smooth the rake heaps into rainproof haycocks. It was unbearably lonesome, hot work by myself with father cutting or raking in other dry sloughs. If only mother with Mabel would come over the rise in some magical way, how relieved with happiness I would be. But no!

I amused myself one evening by imitating the cries of coyotes on the ridge. I did so well that father hurried to me in fear I was being attacked. Lifting their heads to the sky their cry is weird, very like a heart-broken abandoned or grief-stricken woman's cry. So I imagine mine would be if I were left alone without any hope in this great emptiness.

The afternoon air was scorching hot, stiflingly oppressive, the sky a shimmery blue with a dark copper fan cloud gathering in the west. Suddenly,a strong, roaring wind came at us out of the vastness. Anxiously we ran for the shelter of a load of hay, driving the oxen with difficulty, father at their head, I prodding the rear. The storm of hail broke in mad fury as if the pent-up anger of the gods were wreaking vengeance at our invading of the undisputed territory. When we arrived at camp, father was minus his hat, with a red handkerchief tied under his whiskers, two large lumps on his head from the hail, my sunbonnet battered to pulp and a bruised shoulder; a sorry sight we were, yet we laughed and gathered large hail stones to eke out our water supply, spreading our bedding to dry in the warm sun as it returned, chasing the storm war-horses before its beams.

Early in the morning before sun up, and that *is* early, father arose to attend to the oxen. He returned shortly with consternation in every fibre to tell me the oxen were gone, "to hasten breakfast." In the clearer light of sun-up we found their tracks in the wet grass toward the east. We traced them through long, grassy miles home. Mother had them in the kraal. Startled by a noise she found Berry standing looking in at her. They had tasted a bit of everything in the garden before making their presence known. How very contrary oxen can be!

After a lunch we prepared to return to the haying, Martha accompanying us this time. We were to ride ox-back. Martha chose Berry placing a mat on his back on which to sit. I elected bare-back. Father followed shouldering another pitchfork to show how hay fields were mown. In a few miles I found myself slipping forward. Suddenly over onto Bright's neck, grabbing his horns, I yelled. Father, prodding with a fork behind, sent Bright off on a wild run. Finally in much merriment we halted and I again adjusted on ox-back. Bright's horns were so wide that I, astride, could not have jumped clear of him, so it is well I stuck to his horns and to him.

When we reached camp the sun was setting in mighty splashes of purple crimson flames lengthening the light to make camp. Martha and I slept on the load of hay away from the buzz and torment of constant mosquito hosts. We sang "The Spacious Firmament on High" for worship and so to rest after a long, tiring day.

Next morning we moved camp. While I was making the fire Martha unloaded the camp equipment, throwing the lid of the tin trunk (which held our food) on my head. As if there was no other spot in all this lone land for a lid to be hurled! With camphor to disinfect, the bleeding was stopped. Father lectured on carelessness, that nearly all accidents were from carelessness. Before the sun went down we remembered mother's oft-repeated, "Never let the sun go down upon your wrath." So peace reigned supreme in this ageless, vastest, limitless, space.

Sometimes we do get lonesome, Grandma.

Our love,

Maryanne.

*D*ear *Grandma,*

The week (we were haying — I wrote you, remember?) we caught some ducks in the pin-feather stage, unable to fly. These we cleaned, skinned and boiled for a meal. We were indeed glad when father announced that haying was finished and we could break camp for home. This we joyously did, for home sweet home, for mother, John, Jen and Mabel were there. As we walked behind the wagon loaded with hay a big badger ran under a wheel, though only three wheels there was plenty of room elsewhere. As it was hurt we killed it, skinning it at home, stretching the hide on the north side of the shanty. Mother roasted it for the oil for future use. The meat was white and looked like good young porker.

Martha and I were refreshing ourselves with a drink of homemade vinegar with soda for a fizz. In our scramble to prevent me having the second drink we upset the jar bringing mother's annoyance upon us.

This week, Parenteau's of Gabriel's Crossing, about 45-50 miles down the river, called here on their way home from visiting exiled Gabriel Dumont in Montana. They had a band of ponies. Father looked them over and traded the Goodwin heifer for a fleet-footed high-spirited black pony. She is supposed to have blood of famous "Fire-Fly." We call her Fly. There was a lovely brass studded, plaited leather bridle on her, but the next morning it had disappeared, vanished in the night. The traders must have regretted leaving it with us and rather than ask for it, sneaked it away. Though they got a pure-bred, unregistered Shorthorn in the trade.

Canon Flett, of Prince Albert school, said when I was a bit older he would have a school for me to teach. We are to have a school in the spring. He saw our lost sheep. He had shot some chickens and left them hanging in a bluff about nine miles away. They will be high on his return but that is the way he likes them, he says.

The uncles have a reaper, which cuts the grain on to an apron where it slides to the ground. We followed the reaper with mother binding the sheaves. You take a handful of the straw, divide it in two, wrap your hand about it, twisting the ends together and under.

Then we gathered the sheaves in long stooks up and together, with two sheaves on top, to shed any rain there might be. We pulled the peas. They were so ripe we had to spread quilts and sheets on the wagon rack as they burst at a mere touch. Father cradled the barley.

One bright blue noon we had just finished pulling the flax when we were surprised to hear an unusual deep loud whistle from the river. Off we scampered just in time to see a steam-boat going by down the river, probably to Lake Winnipeg and on to Winnipeg city. We were quite delighted to know that there was some life, that we were yet living and not alone.

Father pitched the wheat sheaves on the wagon rack. Martha and I placed them as directed in rows heads to centre. When we reached home we unloaded where the stable will be. Father pitched off the sheaves while I built them into a stack. Round and round to the centre, trying to keep the outside straight, topping off to a taper and fastened with a stake. It was a bit lop-sided but the first I ever built or saw, as in Palmerston at Uncle Sandy's they do not build stacks but put the sheaves into a big barn to await the threshing with their horses to go round and round. Mother has not been very well lately, though busy. The night was beautiful

with a harvest moon, when we heard the creak of freighters'
outfits in the distance. Father sent me to the trail on the run
to ask them if they had any liquor they could part with, as
mother was ill. Two of the men returned with me bringing
some brandy, for which they accepted some eggs and father's
gratitude for supplying our need.

We were hunting along the river for the two ponies when
we found loaded bushes of black currants, which we picked.
Later, when getting the ponies, we saw farther up the river
several of the cattle deep in water. Upon investigating, there
were seven head — Uncle Joe's oxen Cap and Major, with five
cows. They were unable to budge, so away I speeded to where
the men were plowing to tell them of what seemed a dire
catastrophe. With horses and our oxen (for once not driving
us to despair) chains, planks, ropes, axes and shovels then
men hurried to the scene of action. It seems very strange that
in all the long twisted miles of the Saskatchewan river these
cattle had to choose this one quicksand spot for a drink and
coolness from mosquitoes, big flies, and gnats, although if
you rubbed underneath them your hand dripped blood.
Martha and I brought lunch and kept a fire for a smudge and
to warm the men as stripped to the waist in the cool water
they occasionally came out to warm. They tried to dam the
water with planks and to pry under the beasts, then put a
plank under to prevent them from slipping or sinking out of
sight altogether. Finally they could work rope under and
about them, these ropes and chains fastened to a whiffle-tree

on our oxen; with many haws, gees, whoa-haws, at length each beast was released from the suction. On the last haul father twisted his arm.

In rather an angry sunset we hastened the cattle home after what seemed an endless anxious day. Mother had been summoned to a sickbed. Martha was sure mother would return to Palmerston. But where was the money coming from for the railway fare from Moose Jaw and how would she get to the railway; one cannot fly without a feather! Tired, hungry and very desolate we did our belated chores. Presently mother came home to tell us we had another cousin; we did not enthuse much or care so long as we had dear mother to ourselves again.

That night the wind howled loud and long trying to blow us out of the place, dust over everything. The grass floor is worn down so that the rain forms islands from which we hop to the next. Mabel is afraid to try to walk so we put her on the table to teach her with more confidence in herself on the level.

Next morning I was out on blind pony to bring the cattle home. When they came to the ravine they became unmanageable to me, running every way up the bank towards home. Brownie our collie had now deserted me for her pups though I had coaxed her away for miles with an occasional treat of bread. Sitting disconsolately, crying in my despair, I was provoked to see Uncle Rob witness my helplessness. But he gave a glance at me, a shout to the cattle; they took notice of him as he readily rounded them up, scrambling for all they were able. We had not located them the night previous and we are glad to have milk again. I could not be cross with Brownie.

Love, from

Maryanne.

———— ◆ ————

*D*ear *Grandma,*

We are very fond of our wild geese that hatched from the eggs we found in the spring. They are very tame and great company, following us about as they proudly wend their way from shack, kraal, well and sods, chattering continuously as if to lose no opportunity of impressing their stories of captivity. They are stately gentlemen dressed in grey and black formal suits with a black tie, or it may be a black bandage, tied under the chin for sore throat, from talking too much. They sit down beside you and commence to chatter, move and they are there again.

I rode our pony "Fly," in quest of the lost sheep. Every few miles Fly would suddenly jump to one side startled so I would find myself on the ground with a thump and a thud. What Indian ghost did she see? She did this five times during our 52-mile ride. At first I was terrified that she might run away and that I might be left all alone far from home on this stretch of trackless prairie. Though Fly shied and I could not always hang on to her mane, or the pad (for a saddle) she would run a few yards, stop and take a few bites, then let me come to her and again mount. Once when I was longer in getting up, she came and nosed me. I took the bridle reins, and nursed my injuries.

Nevertheless she is a darling and so readily taught. If we touch her on the shoulder she lowers herself and we dismount. Again if we want to mount, touch her with three taps on the knees with a switch and she is on her knees to let you mount. Others do not approve of our having her and when they get horses they will be "stallion-mares" if you know what they are – Clydesdales.

About 25 miles down the river from home I located the sheep, but the minute the pesky creatures spied us they stood motionless, then turned and bolted north with all possible speed, just jumping bunches of wool in the distance. It seemed impossible for me to get ahead to turn them home-wards. The late afternoon shadows were lengthening when tired, sore and disgusted I turned Fly westward till we came to the old rutted cart trail and then south. It is well we have the river on the east for a guide. The old cart trails have at least a dozen ruts running parallel north and south. The traders no doubt had extra ponies tied to the side of the carts or two or three carts alongside if they had less men than carts. At times we can hear the creak, squeak of the wooden carts several miles away but seldom see them at close view or range.

There is to be a fair at Saskatoon and Aunt Frankie has asked mother to let her take us to it, though we have not much to exhibit and we are needed at home. Mother got us ready, making starch from potatoes for our white petticoats. I made a hat for myself with a piece left from my wine dress Aunt Belle had made for me. I folded the goods over a straw crown and put three pom-poms on in front.

Martha's hat, I made from a piece of muskrat fur about the rim. We had killed the muskrat on the plowing near the slough. Jen had a guinea fowl feather in her grey lamb cap. Our winter clothing is to come in the loads from Moose Jaw.

We were up in the middle of the night and arrived in the bleak, grey dawn at Uncle Rob's. Aunt Frankie inspected us. Into the wagon we put mother's cheese and butter, rhubarb stalks, a jar of dried periwinkle peas and some of father's White Russian wheat. Martha had drawn a map of Canada and done some of her fine writing. It ought to be, for she is provokingly at it, in the sand or drops of water, any place at all.

I did a scene of the pony feeding on the river bank and a cart nearby, using the bluebag, dandelion coloring, beet-juice and some spinach green from the garden. It is an awful daub, but Aunt Frankie had made a fine white shirt, crochetted lace and a pair of woollen cuffs for father and some of her fancy work.

The day broke lovely and clear. On our way we had lunch at the camping spot beyond the big ravine near the river. The fair was held in a "lean-to" adjoining Mrs. Fletcher's store, in which they hold school other days. We went out around to see what was to be seen. We found Uncle Joe and told him of the telegram the day before that Grandpa Caswell had died.

There were a number of Sioux Indians with their carts and ponies camped in teepees down by the river near Marrs' and Kerr's. There was an Indian pony race and squaw race, which we enjoyed.

The day was now bleak, with a cold wind. We met the Hunter girls sitting on some calves to warm themselves, (also) the English lady, Mrs. Prendergast, and her daughter, Muriel, to whom this country must seem strange if we are to believe our geography. Though she lost her son (he was drowned while she was on the way out to join him), she has one relation (Horne) at whose home we cooked our bacon on the last day of our trip in May. We also met the Powe girls and Sandy Marrs and then returned to the fair and Aunt Frankie.

We got a few prizes, and Uncle Joe prizes on the cattle. Mrs. Fletcher took us with her to have supper. There were a number of guests: her sister, Mrs. Cap Andrews, the Clark girls and the Goodwin boys and Will and Fred Bates. Mrs. Kerr came to see us about the dance and what the ladies would wear. Dulmage's girls have an organ and can play it. She gave us a piece of her prize cake with "Taste and See" decorations made from high bush red cranberry taffy or jelly. Looked too good to eat.

In the evening there was a dance at the school room when the fair things were all cleared out. We sat on benches trying our best to keep awake and look interested. I think the fiddlers were Charlie Blackley and Will Haley. We liked the "Waltz Buddrille" and "Drops of Brandy" or Rabbitt Dance. Finally Aunt Frankie's brother, Will Irvine (who is a miller but a mill where?) drove us out to his homestead. Glad at last to stretch our weary, sleepy selves on the bed on the floor, where we had plenty of room, we slept soundly till long after sun-up.

After breakfast we returned to Saskatoon where Uncle John was ready to return to Clark's Crossing, home, and mother. Aunt Frankie remained in Saskatoon to visit her sister Katie, and other friends, particularly Mrs. Cap Andrews from Alliston.

Much love, from

Maryanne.

$\mathscr{D}$*ear Grandma,*

We had news through Molloys, that Uncle Rob had secured a job as telegraph relief officer at Banff, in the mountains. Aunt Frankie came home to pack up. Miss Blackley and Miss Elliott came with her to visit and help in the packing.

A Mr. Hamilton arrived, too, to have service or church. As this was the first we all went to Uncle Rob's in our wooden-legged wagon, the frost and the moonlight making it a radiant scene. We sang "Crown Him, Crown Him" after the psalms and prayers. Mother was very sad at parting for we are going to miss Aunt Frankie and Wallace, who is lots of fun. Mother wishing we had gone to Vancouver as her cousins McLeans urged father to do, even coming from "The Sanble" to try to influence father, but he was for N.W.T. Anyway, at Moose Jaw we could have had a school, though now we do try to spell, recite and do sums, but time is so very scarce.

There does not seem to be time to burn the limekiln to build our concrete house that has been planned, so it has been decided to build a black brick one of wiry prairie sod plowed from the edge of the slough toward the river. After the place for it was staked out, father plowed the sods and cut them with a spade into uniform lengths of about two feet or more. Then we loaded them onto the stoneboat, drawn by the oxen. At the staked place, we helped unload and place them in proper position; every second row the join of the lower sods being overlapped by the next top one, father shifting where necessary to keep the walls straight and plumbed. The walls are three sods thick. The door and a window in the east, a large window in the south, a door jamb in the west filled with sods, but to be removed in the spring and a milk house built on to the main building. For rafters we used poplar poles. For floor, sleepers and ceiling beams, scantling from an old scow we found down the river. For concrete ceiling-floor, the boards from the shanty. It was early on a cold windy morning when we tore it down, praying there would be no rain or snow till we were ready.

Straw or hay was spread on the willows nailed to the rafters and then we were ready for placing sods on the roof, overlapping them as shingles to make the roof weatherproof. We built beds of pole-posts, and lumber. Mother tacked new rag carpet to the wall and a post to make bedrooms with sheets, bureau and cupboards dividing to make the living room. We have no parlor. We made small pegs and drove them into the wall at regular intervals in a straight line down to the floor, then tacked brown building paper lengthwise on to the pegs, putting boards around for a baseboard. This will keep the dust from sifting. Father made a sundial on the floor, so we will know the time of day. We have one outside, too.

Uncle Joe made a trip to Prince Albert with our wagon wheel, for repairs, so that now we are fairly comfortable. Father and he left again for Moose Jaw for food supplies and our household goods. Mother baked all the flour into bread for the trip on the long trail, saving one loaf for Mabel. Mother made a flail of two sticks, a long and a shorter one, holes bored in an end of each, then tied a bit of shagginappi through the holes, loosely. With this, the long piece for a

handle, we beat wheat heads on to a sheet, cleaned it of chaff in the wind, washed it and then boiled for a long time to eat with milk and a pinch of salt and sugar. It is very good. Some of the wheat we took turns grinding in the coffee mill for porridge, sifting some for johnny cake, as the corn meal is all used. We have plenty of other food but no bread.

Father had shot some wild geese with the musket before he left. There are great flocks of them resting on the sand bars and shores of the river. At night we hear the incessant chit-chatter of them. Early in the morning before dawn they feed on the stubble, then back to the river in kite formation. Again about noon and four o'clock they come, standing as thick in a line as poles of a stockaded fort.

Uncle John took the mare and colt for a screen. Just as he fired the shot, the colt jumped into line. With the one shot he killed the colt and five geese. He was frantic with annoyance. Of course he got many more wild geese and had to clip the wings of our tamed wild geese as they have shown a great longing to fly away. How lonely we should be without our companions!

Down on the stubble where we had the peas and flax and rye, Uncle John shot one of two tall, beautiful white and buff cranes. The fluffy feathers under the tail were wonderfully pretty and soft like swan's down.

We helped Uncle John finish our stable, or Uncle John helped us. It, too, is built of sods as we did the house. We children all went to the ravine with the pony. We cut willow brush (to put on the rafters), tied a rope about the butt end, then to the whiffle-tree, for the pony to haul home. Then, when ready for many trips, we spread hay for a roof. We have poles for mangers and stalls, like Mr. Wilson's at Beaver Creek. In one corner, a pen for the sheep and another for turnips, potatoes and roots. Adjoining outside is the hen house, with cotton for a window.

We topped the turnips, gathered the vegetables, storing some in the hole under the floor for a cellar.

"Canary Smiths" stayed two nights with us, on their way to Prince Albert from Saskatoon, for the winter. As it had snowed slightly mother asked the boy if he would take our pony and bring home our lost sheep. They could be readily traced in the snow. In the evening we discerned them coming

and went to meet them. Without much difficulty we got them into the pen we had made, again rejoicing another worry was over for a while.

Father is still in Moose Jaw.

Love, from

Maryanne.

———— ◆ ————

*D*ear *Grandma,*

Father and Uncle Joe had been gone three weeks, all but a day, when on a beautiful, clear, frosty Saturday night we heard the creak of the wagons five miles away. Thrilled, we hastily donned coats, caps, mitts, and away to meet them. Imagine our longing for bread when our greetings were shouts, "Have you any bread?" We raided the grub-box.

Father was alone as Uncle Joe had stayed in Saskatoon. By the time we reached home the moon had an opal ring about it predicting change in the weather. After we had all shared a late supper we began to unload the wagons, stowing some goods under the beds, others on the loft of the ceiling to store, and also to prevent the boards from warping as they are not nailed.

One big box of goods was open, contents soaking wet. We spread them to dry. The water at the Saskatoon ferry was low with a large sand bar near the west bank. The ferry took loads, and teams were driven across the sandbar. The goods were unloaded into a boat, rowed then to the shore, while the teams and empty wagons were driven into the icy water. The teams, swimming amid great chunks of ice, dragged the wagon, but when the big box was put into the boat it was too large and tipped off into the river. Somehow it burst but the men with pike poles rescued it and most of the contents, though we cannot find our skates. We are surmising mother took them out before the packing was finished.

While we were busy with the loads mother made a big batch of sour milk biscuits; though it was Sunday by the clock, this seemed as necessary as the Sabbath stories of the Bible for "we were an hungered."

We went to bed happier and more content than we had been since our arrival. Father was well pleased with our efforts in accomplishing so many things in the time he was away, but the weather had helped us too. It had been clear and mild. Early Sunday, though tired, we were astir. The storm had come whirling and swirling like foam in great fury. We did our chores and then went to Uncle John's and the others for dinner before we had our Sunday service. The Prince Albert branch of the Dawson tele-graph is quite close to us and Uncle John's so we had it for a guide in the snow. They came through the storm although it was not cold.

Monday it had cleared. Tuesday the sun had melted most of the snow. We went to the river to water the stock and get a barrel of water. While there we spied Uncle Joe with the pole in hand crossing the river on a block of ice jumping from one block to another pushing his way across till finally he reached shore. We were frightened but excited with relief breathing freely again. The ferry had been taken out of the river after our loads. He came down on the other side leaving the team at Lakes of the stone house, till later.

We had wonderful sights this week watching, at night, the whole country across the river one great blaze of towering flames, as it came closer, leaping and dancing in mad delight, roaring and racing for hundreds of unhindered miles to quench its thirst at the river's edge when, in wild, fantastic leaps, it died, succumbed. But oh! That next morning what a blackened desolate country was our eastern view. We much preferred the golden glow of the prairie grass and were glad when later in the week snow covered the scarred scene. In the spring there will be miles of fresh green grass from here to Humboldt and possibly to Qu'Appelle.

We have never seen anything like the fascinating Aurora Borealis or Northern Lights. The whole heaven at times is lit up with these uncanny lights, dancing in and out, whimsically up and down, in variegated sheets of colors of the rainbow. Once this fall they were as if the heavens were an umbrella splotched with red ink from the centre running in rivulets to the horizon, caught up and away again as if in measured time of notes. There's beauty here, Grandma.

Love,

Maryanne.

---

*D*ear Grandma,

Some Indians from White Caps reserve above Saskatoon called on their way to visit their Sioux friends across the North Saskatchewan at Prince Albert. They had a wooden cart with a frame of sticks about the floor of it for a rack. The squaws sat jouncing on the bottom. A pony was hitched in the pole shafts. An Indian rode another pony ahead. Trailing behind was a dog hitched to a breast strap, with two light poles on either side on which was a piece of canvas stretched between. On this were some kettles and bundles. The poles, like shafts, dragged on the ground. This vehicle is called a *travois*. These Indians were quite interested watching mother as she walked back and forth spinning the carded wool we need for yarn for stockings and mitts.

The papoose was cute, strapped in a moss-filled bag on a board with a frame above its face for protection. It rode on its mother's back. Mother gave it a pair of Mabel's stockings. When they return we hope they will have bead work to trade.

Then on Sunday morning, while we were on our knees at prayers, a tall Indian walked in without knocking with a string of prairie chickens. He spoke Cree and wanted flour in exchange for the chickens. He kept saying, "ne moi yali" which means "no," Warren Finlayson told us that afternoon when he came from the telegraph office to visit. His father is Indian agent at Mistawasis and Warren is learning to operate the telegraph board. These Indians had dogs hitched to a closed-in toboggan and ran behind the dogs cracking a whip and yelling at them.

We two girls take turns getting up in the middle of the night to light the fire and to feed the oxen so father can get away early or late in the night to return before dark in the evening with a load of hay from ten miles away. When he returns about sundown, 3:30-4:00 p.m., we unhitch and feed the oxen while he has a warm drink; then father pitches off the hay on to the roof of the stable and we roll it near the manhole to push it into the alley below when we feed the stock later. Next year we will have a fence to protect the hay from the stock.

We have built a sort of shed with poplar poles and willow brush about the grain stacks, leaving one side white next to the stable. On this enclosure we smoothed the snow

and threw water to make a hard frozen surface. While
father is away for hay or wood, we throw down sheaves of
wheat and ride the pony over them to trample the wheat
out of the heads, then fork the straw, after several turnings,
to the chickens to scratch and keep them busy. If the straw
is not sufficiently cleaned of wheat, we use the flail and trot
the pony again. When satisfied, we scoop it up on to sheets
and quilts spread in the open to be fanned by the wind to
remove the chaff. In our spare time we pick the best and
largest kernels for next spring's prized Russian seed-wheat.

We do the chores, cut or saw the wood into stove lengths
and are glad that our stove fire-box is such a very long
one. An Englishman named Barley suggested we just shove one
end of the pole into the fire-box and as it burned, shove
again. We are not lazy.

The days are getting very short and to help our coal-oil
eke out we have used a "witch-light," which is a rag on a
button in a saucer with some tallow in it to burn, but this
week we helped thread the wick into candle moulds. We
put a double thread of wick down through the hole at the
bottom and after pulling a small stick through the loops at
the top we pull down and knot the ends at the bottom to
hold and keep the melted tallow from dripping. When hard-
ened we cut the knots off, warm mould slightly, draw on the
stick and there are the candles, much preferred to any
"witch-light." Jen made spills of paper to save the matches.

Everybody works at something all the while. John carries
in the wood and snow, gathers the eggs and feeds the chickens.

Jen helps mother with the house-work and plays with Mabel. Martha and I out of doors choring.

We're all well, Grandma.

Love, from

Maryanne.

———— • ————

*D*ear *Grandma,*

A Mr. George Barley stopped overnight on his way to Prince Albert. He has a team of mules. He has built a round stone house on his homestead about ten or more miles upriver. Says he built it round so there will be no dirt in the corners. He has been trying to arrange with father to work with or for us next spring. Wears his hair long and does not shave. Says Jesus wore his hair and whiskers as he does and that is the style for him.

The river was frozen over. Gladly we went with father for a load of wood and to do some measuring of the river from bank to bank to locate a likely place for a railway bridge when it comes, as we are not far from "MacKenzie's survey." Father's friend, Mr. Archibald Young of Toronto, has written him for this information. We felt quite elated and important to do this and made our first winter picnic of it.

We built a fire while father selected and cut the trees, then we lopped off the smaller branches and helped load the sleigh. When the water was boiling in the camp kettle we put in a pinch of tea, toasted our frozen sandwiches of bread and cheese stuck on sticks over the coal. After refreshments we started our measurements across up and down the river each trip until we had covered several miles. Father later sent his measurements to Mr. Young. An acknowledgment came from his son at Upper Canada College to say his father had passed on. The loss of his friend was a great blow to father.

A letter came this mail to inform the Caswells that their mother's brother, Thomas Dickson, had died in Denver, Colo., leaving an estate without a will. When we receive our share we girls are to go to the convent at Prince Albert. We are getting ready now.

We made some Christmas cards to send to our relatives and friends in Ontario. We peeled and dried some birch bark off some of the wood pieces from the river bank. We selected our best pressed and dried flowers that had retained their coloring, pasting them with egg white in a pleasing arrangement or design, sometimes stitching them. The spring flowers and autumn made the best showing, but we are anxious to display the variety that grew on the wild prairies, so each family got different flowers and colorings. It was a problem to get white paper to wrap the finished cards for mailing, so we wrapped them in yellow-brown building paper for security, and note paper for addressing. We were complimented on the results, so we are making some for our walls.

Father has been to Duck Lake stone grist-mill with wheat made into flour and some cracked for porridge and johnny cake. It takes a long time grinding in the little hand coffee mill. We are sending a pair of Black Spanish fowl to Mr. McKenzie, the miller, for their kind hospitality of the open trail to father. On the way he found a large seven-pronged antler, which we have fastened on the wall to hang our head gear of hoods and caps.

For Christmas gifts we had not any (like Simple Simon) but we exchanged some of our treasures and put them on a bare poplar tree, decorated some Chautauqua books Uncle Alex or A. K. had sent us with his usual Christmas letter. "May the Lord bless you and keep you and make his face to shine upon you and do you good."

For dinner we had a cherished wild goose stuffed with potato dressing seasoned with wild sage, vegetables, of course, suet pudding of grated carrots, flour and dried saskatoon berries boiled in a cloth.

Mother allowed us some hoarded sugar for taffy, flavored with wild mint. Some of our pop-corn popped but not much pop in it. We danced on the threshing floor and in the evening played hide-and-seek and did some story reading by lamp for a treat as coal-oil is five dollars a gallon at Saskatoon.

At midnight Christmas Eve we girls went to the stable to see if the oxen would kneel as father said they would or did on Christmas Eve. We had never had the opportunity until now. When mother followed us out to the stable the oxen knelt for a second, as they got up they were disturbed. See?

We missed you and our old friends, Grandma. Everyone sends love.

Maryanne.

———◆———

January 1, 1888

$\mathcal{D}$ear Grandma,

Next day was dull and mild. Father had gone for hay. We were returning from the river water-hole with the cattle when we saw flames leaping from the stove-pipe in the roof of our sod house. We ran with all speed. Mother was just finishing the wash and could not believe us as the fire was low. But as the sight soon convinced her she threw salt into the stove, sent Martha to the roof while Jen and John carried water to me at the ladder, Martha getting it to the top. We finally, with salt, water, beating and stuffing with a mat, got it under control. Mother's strength then seemed to desert her. When father came there was a discussion of ways and means to build a chimney for safety and to stop the continual dripping of soot.

We got in a barrel, filled it with frozen clay dug from the well, as this thawed we spaded it fine and mixed with chaff. Father made a brace for the chimney so we have a book shelf, and a place for the water pail below. We carried the mixed clay while father each night added a bit till finished.

We have heaps of snow and it has stormed several days. Father always goes to inspect the stock just before bedtime. This night mother put on her shawl and followed him. In a few minutes father burst in to us with, "See what I found." Behind him we saw mother smiling. Then father said, "Oh it's you. Not a strange woman lost in the storm."

Nearing the stable, he had met a strange man who said, "Guess I am lost but the team seemed to know where they were heading." Just then mother appeared on the scene. Father said, "Oh you poor man, lost, and a woman with you. Unhitch while I take this frozen woman back to the house. I'll be back in a minute. Come away with me to the house. Be careful of these steps in this snowbank." Mother smiled, no chance to explain.

The man was Al Lafond whom Uncle John had just hired and had been for hay. Father did not recognize or know him and in the storm did not see the load of hay. Surprised and excited he jumped to the conclusion of lost travellers in the storm and no refuge for miles unless the river. How mother teased! Al spent the night with us. New Year's (Sunday) service today.

Last night at midnight, father went out and fired off the musket into the air. Uncle Joe, on his way to celebrate, shot a rabbit, which he left for us. Mother and I like rabbit, but the others, ugh! For dinner mother cooked the last of our salted cod fish, potatoes in their skin, dried raspberries, cooked or stewed johnny cake.

Before dark we found a new calf in the stable so now we will have plenty of milk in the new year though another cow dropped dead on the way to the river yesterday.

It is shovelling snow, bucking, cutting or sawing wood, mending ox-harness, setting and sharpening the bucksaw, driving cattle to the river watering-hole, cutting and cleaning it out, hauling water out of the well, feeding the stock, cleaning the stable and chicken house, riding the pony on the threshing floor, helping unload hay, teaching the pups to heel and "lie down dead," reading out loud in the firelight, seeing pictures in the flames, off to bed and sleep to be up early to begin the new year of 1888. What will it have for us?

Happy New Year to all.

Your

Maryanne.